COMING HOME
peace without complacency

MARGARET RANDALL

COMING HOME
peace without complacency

MARGARET RANDALL

west end press
1990

First printing
ISBN 0-931122-57-0

Printed in the United States of America

Cover photograph by Margaret Randall. Except where specifically
credited, all inside photographs by Margaret Randall.
Typography by Prototype.
Design by Michael Reed.

West End Press
P.O. Box 27334
Albuquerque, NM 87125

TABLE OF CONTENTS

Coming Home: Peace Without Complacency

COMING HOME:
Peace Without Complacency

I think I was a teenager, but I may have been older during a passionate discussion among my father, mother, and myself. In any case, it's one of the few family events about which all three of us retain similar memory. We were driving somewhere, and I think it was my mother who mentioned a current news item: the ACLU's defense of some neo-Nazi organization's right to hold a public rally. My father regularly contributed to the ACLU, my mother was of liberal persuasion as well, and I had been brought up in this middle-class, white, second-generation American family to believe that defense of difference was an important part of the national conscience.

But there was no agreement in this particular discussion. My mother thought defense of *any* rights for fascists was unthinkable. "If a group advocates hate and killing," as far as she was concerned, "they can *have* no rights!" With all my youthful passion, I agreed. My father, against both of us—who could usually talk faster and turn a more intricate phrase than he could—was adamant in his defense. He hated anything fascist as much as we did. But this would cease to be a democracy, he kept saying, unless we make sure we defend *everyone's* freedom of expression.

A week or so after the victory in my struggle against the U.S. Immigration and Naturalization Service (INS), the memory of this old argument surfaced. The experience of hard years of fighting deportation has taught me a great deal. If it wasn't absolutely clear to me before, censorship, as a vehicle for so-called protection, has become increasingly repugnant. The government attempted to exclude me because of my ideas. I continue to believe

1

that human beings must be allowed, in fact encouraged, to express our ideas and feelings—in all their plenitude and difference.

Today I can better understand my father's plea. But something of my mother's point of view continues to speak, insistent in my gut. If freedom is important to us, we must fight against the spread of a fascist ideology in every way open to us; so it's hard for me to defend *everyone's* rights. It's hard for me to defend the rights of racist and other hate groups to promote their corrupt and corrupting world views.

Certainly, given a constitution like ours, we must struggle so that its protection extends to the commonly disenfranchised, not just to those in power. But that's the key question: *who holds the power?* If the power is held, as it is in this country, by a bourgeois minority within a context of class exploitation, then the powerless shouldn't have to worry about protecting the interests of those who already have all the power. The powerful are quite capable of protecting themselves.

And what about the fascists? some would ask. The American Nazi party and the Ku Klux Klan don't govern this country (though the latter certainly holds a dangerous measure of power). I guess there my bottom-line response is that in a life-and-death struggle —which I have no doubt we are waging, on all sorts of fronts—we must consistently choose life if we hope to survive.

I'm troubled by instances of censorship within certain socialist societies. If they are truly workers' states, how can the accessibility of a range ideas be closed to working people? Denied the opportunity to discuss opposing views, how can we learn to think for ourselves, to develop our own convictions? Perhaps this is not really a censorship issue, but one of how functional (in this arena, at least) the workers' society in question really is.

Frequently, in countries whose territorial integrity is being threatened, there are also extenuating circumstances: in wartime, certain types of censorship may be necessary, even when they are not desirable, and this necessity may be heightened as well by the fact that a small country is struggling against the multiple pressures of a much larger power. Socialism, even in peacetime, defines itself as a transitional society. Capitalism proudly asserts it is the best there is.

So, I would argue, censorship is to be avoided wherever possible, but it's never exercised in a vacuum. Censorship by and for (or against) whom? In each case, context and the interests served must inform the answer.

Working within a bourgeois democracy, we are too easily trapped by the myth that all views are honored. The myth encourages ordinary men and women to respect this principle, while those who govern continue to abuse our rights. I don't think I would actively support the ACLU in its defense of the "rights" of hate-mongers, although I certainly support that organization's defense of issues and people I respect. Faced with a neo-Nazi rally today, I wouldn't actively promote its freedom of expression, but neither would I propose that it be suppressed. Instead, I would attempt to mobilize everyone I could to the understanding that such anti-human views mean death to us all.

What I know without a doubt is that there are other ways in which we can, and must, struggle against fascism in America. We must retrieve our common histories, educate, alert, and mobilize: against fascism and racism, nuclear irresponsibility, the so-called right to life ideology, destruction of our earth and atmosphere, privilege for the rich, blind protection for the powerful, sexism, homophobia, homelessness, ignorance, and exploitation and oppression of all kinds.

A great deal of what I know about the importance of freedom of expression and freedom of dissent I have learned from personal day-in and day-out experience over the past five years, since the U.S. Immigration and Naturalization Service issued a deportation order against me because of my ideas—the nature of some of my books, and my refusal to retreat from my position, that of my constitutionally protected right to think, write, speak, and teach what I believe.

I am one of millions. Millions of women and men who espouse hundreds of differing ideas about the nature of society, history, the changes we believe would improve the life of our planet. I am not a member of the ruling elite. I didn't write the laws—protecting many of us on paper, but in truth only the governing few. I learned that I must fight for my right to be heard, included, respected; and I must fight for the rights of others.

I SOME HISTORY

In 1961, at the age of 24, I left New York City and went to Mexico. I already considered myself a writer (I wrote a lot of romantic poetry, and had completed a very bad first novel); and expressed incipient left political views—more radical than those of my family and, I should add, most of my artist friends. I was also a single mother; my son Gregory was born in October of 1960.

The sixties in Mexico had something in common with the sixties elsewhere. Poets and writers in general began talking to one another through a laborious network of independent readings, broadsides, little magazines, presses, and forums. Student-led protest movements erupted in the wake of the Cuban Revolution; 1968 would produce Mexico City's own version of New York's Columbia University, or May in Paris. Mexico had invested heavily in hosting the 1968 Olympic Games, though, and a repressive government couldn't afford to see that invesment lost; at the Plaza of Three Cultures, more than a thousand unarmed demonstrators were massacred on October 2nd, an event that would change that country's history—and mine.

In early 1962, Mexican poet Sergio Mondragon and I began editing a bilingual literary magazine which was to provide a coming together for the most exciting new voices of North and Latin America. The journal, which was called *El Corno Emplumado* (*The Plumed Horn*), proposed a bridge—between the plumes of Quetzalcoatl and the jazz horn of the United States. And it echoed our own development through those years, starting as an eclectic showcase for young writers and artists and eventually becoming a more cohesive mirror of work by intellectuals on both continents, in most cases creative thinkers and activists who were deeply concerned with injustice and directed our creativity toward change.

There was intense correspondence, now spanning five continents. There was an increasing interest and energy put into translation: We wanted to make our work available to one another, in all its formal subtleties as well as in its content. We sponsored and attended gatherings of young nonconformist artists and writers. With our energy and exuberance, we believed we could change the world.

Cuba was essential; today it is *chic* to espouse long-distance views on that country's successes and failures, but it would be impossible here to overemphasize the impact made by the Cuban Revolution on the lives of generations of Latin Americans. Quite simply, David reenacted his struggle with Goliath. A tiny island nation had shown the world that it was possible to stand up to the United States, reclaiming its identity and dignity. My first trip there, to a gathering of poets in 1967, and another in 1968, for a meeting of more than six hundred Third World intellectuals, had a lasting effect on my outlook. In a complex and profound sense, my own life and work were becoming a *bridge*.

During the Mexican years Sergio Mondragon and I were married. We had two daughters, Sarah and Ximena. There was a

4

great cultural richness in the early life of this new family of five. Sergio brought to our relationship the Quetzalcoatl myth, the bird rising above its conquerors; I brought the quick though perhaps somewhat innocent energy of New York streets, the new Beat consciousness of North America. But the construction began to come apart over time. My husband moved toward certain Eastern philosophies while I moved further to the left. Our daily sustenance depended increasingly upon my efforts.

As a woman in a particularly misogynist society, as a foreigner in Mexico, it was never easy for me to obtain adequate or adequately paid work. In 1966, on the misadvice of a lawyer, I took out Mexican citizenship. It was an economic move, an effort to support my three children (then all under the age of six). I was motivated by the emotional pressure of a marriage and the urgent and practical needs of my family.

In the acquisition of Mexican citizenship, which was completed in 1967, I was under the impression that I had to relinquish my U.S. nationality. Dutifully, I turned my passport over to the American consular authorities. Less than two years later, beginning to understand that Mexican naturalization would make it problematic for me freely to visit my parents and country of origin, I began trying to undo what I unwittingly had done; I attempted through what's known as an administrative recourse to retrieve my U.S. citizenship. Although I had been very clear that economic duress was the reason for the unfortunate switch, the state department turned down my request. They never explained their refusal.

Meanwhile, I continued to grow—as a woman, a writer, an editor, and a politically aware person. Sergio's and my differences became insoluble, and we separated in 1967. I established a relationship with a U.S. poet, Robert Cohen. Our daughter, Ana, was born in 1969. By this time Sergio had also left the magazine, which I continued editing—first alone, and later with Cohen. Feminism hit me, initially, as one more of a series of issues I wanted to embrace, then as a necessary way of connecting the pieces of my own life which had previously seemed so at odds with one another.

In the summer of 1968, the Mexican student movement exploded, held forth for several extraordinary months, then was decimated by repression. Throughout the following year, those of us who publicly protested the death sentence imposed upon that movement began to experience repression of different kinds. The government tried to shut down our magazine, but impressive reader support, from many parts of the world, enabled us to survive. To the regime, our survival must have stung like an open sore. In July of 1969, with my youngest daughter barely three months old, *El Corno* could finally resist no longer. I was forced from any possibility of a normal life in Mexico.

Paramilitary forces came to our home, stole my Mexican passport, and forced me into hiding. The experience of several months of underground life, in which Mexican officialdom always insisted that they knew nothing of what was happening, nor had they anything against me, made it clear I was no longer welcome in that country. My four children traveled to Cuba, where they were lovingly cared for as the Cuban Revolution cared for thousands of children of those engaged in struggle. In September, sick and without papers, I left Mexico. My circumstances made it necessary for me to travel halfway around the world to join my children in Cuba. Robert had arrived there the week before.

I was now in my early thirties. The impact of feminist thought, as well as the experience of national liberation struggles on several fronts and in several stages, turned me toward oral history as a viable means of bridge-building. I wanted to know about women's lives in Cuba and in other parts of the developing world. I wanted to listen to women speak about their lives, about the problems and changes wrought by struggle and sometimes by victory; and I wanted to write books that would offer a context for those women's voices, so they might speak to the people of my own country, the United States.

For I never stopped thinking of the U.S. as my home. In forums and at conferences around the globe, I represented my country of origin. Interviewing women in Vietnam, Nicaraguan women, Chilean women, or women from Peru's jungles and mountains, I was the *gringa* who asked them to talk about what concerned us both—from the unique vision of their lives. Years later I was able to regain my Mexican passport, but I was still a *norteamericana*—a woman of white, middle-class, U.S. roots, from the cultural mix of New Mexico, whose Marxism and even feminism were most often spoken in Spanish, and for whose children that language was their mother tongue. I was a transplant, a hybrid of sorts, who suffered a momentary feeling of confusion when a Puerto Rican TV show host in Boston, in 1978, asked me to tell him how I approached a particular problem "as a North American living in Latin America." Was I really a North American in Latin America, or a Latin American in this country? Or neither? Or both?

After ten years in Cuba, I moved on to Nicaragua. By that time, Robert's and my relationship had disintegrated, and I had lived my last five years in Cuba with a Colombian poet and musician by the name of Antonio Castro. My children were older; one had finished college and the second was about to get her degree. The Sandinistas had won in that Central American country, and once again I was curious—particularly about Nicaraguan women, who had made such a startling contribution to their people's struggle. My old friend Ernesto Cardenal—poet and Catholic priest when I knew him in Mexico—was now also Nicaragua's Minister of Culture. "Come and talk to our women," his invitation read. And I did.

Throughout the years in Cuba, I continued to be a bridge; not only through my own writing—dozens of poems and articles, short stories, books of oral history, and essays on women and culture—but through my translations of important Latin American poets' work. And also by my presence: as a woman, a mother of four, a North American living and working within the revolutionary process. I believed that passion and reason, socialism and feminism, art and responsibility all needed one another, and I wanted to bring them together in my life and work. Members of the Venceremos Brigades, from the first contingent on, and many other travelers as well, would come to visit, and I felt I was able to help translate the Cuban experience in words that respected cultural difference. With the Cubans I was also able to discuss the various idiosyncracies and differing political perspectives of my U.S. sisters and brothers.

This continued in Nicaragua. I was there for three months in late 1979 and early 1980, then returned to live, with my youngest daughter, in December of that year. Soon my second youngest daughter graduated from high school in Cuba, and chose to join us. I was interested in women's lives, in the experience of writers and other cultural workers, and my books from this period reflect that. I was fortunate to have arrived at a time when writers, photographers, and other creative artists were beginning to come together, devising organizational forms which provided infinite new possibilities for our work within a rapidly changing society.

Having lived in a country like Cuba, where the history of church and state had been such an antagonistic one, I also became absorbed in the role of Christians in the Nicaraguan Revolution. This was another bridge, and it drew me—fascinated and energized—to the connections it made. Although they longed for the same peace and justice on earth, believers and nonbelievers had traditionally been pitted against one another by the forces intent on maintaining the status quo, especially in the poorer countries. In Nicaragua, recent history had exploded that myth of "irreconcilable differences."

Again, my family and I were not tourists in the superficial sense. I worked at the Ministry of Culture, for the women's organization and with the media; my children went to local schools; my vantage point was one of engaged participation rather than what the guardians of the "free" press would call impartial observation.

By this time I was doing photography, too. My late entrance into that medium was a way of seeking another bridge: I was frustrated by the language barrier between my poetic expression and my colleagues and friends. The photographic image transcended that barrier. Photography has its own language, though, and I soon began to search for my voice. Most of my books, from the end of the Cuban period on, include my own images as well as my words. More recently, photography has moved beyond illustration in my life; a variety of exhibitions and reproductions in magazines and books attest to that process.

II COMING HOME

I've gone into some detail about my life because I want to share something of where I came from and who I've been in my early years in this country and during my almost quarter century in Latin America. Now I want to speak at greater length about the woman who came home, and what happened when she did.

I lived in Nicaragua for almost four years before returning to the United States in January of 1984. The last couple of years in Managua had been intense. The contra presence was already escalating, as a vehicle of U.S.-backed opposition to the Sandinistas and as a part of its ongoing program of low-intensity warfare against Nicaragua's sovereignty. Many of the innovative and courageous new programs aimed at improving the quality of life for Nicaraguans were suffering as a result. Military attacks in the north and along the southern border were beginning to hit the capital city.

In a nation of young soldiers, I was a woman in my mid-forties—exhausted by years of long hours, with questions about the contribution I was making, needing to come home. Essentially a writer, I knew I had to slow down, to tackle larger and more complex writing projects than those I had been able to complete during my years in Latin America. I believed I no longer had U.S. citizenship, but I had never ceased to think of New Mexico as my special place.

And so I applied for a tourist visa and boarded a plane one morning in Managua's 114° heat. That night I stepped down from another, into the cold of a January evening in Albuquerque. On a reading and lecture tour the year before, I had fallen in love with an old friend, American poet Floyce Alexander. We were writing to one another, and making a life with him as well as moving closer to my parents, brother, and sister were all aspects of the human ties that brought me back. My essential reason, however, was much deeper.

I'm not sure I could have articulated that reason, at least not at first, or not completely. I intuited it, and that was enough. There were those in Nicaragua—among them a psychologist, an exceptional woman named Tony—who had helped me nurture the courage to make the move. They had made me see that following a clear destiny does not by necessity imply denial of the people or places I'd leave behind. Cutting out on a war-torn nation wasn't easy. I didn't want to rationalize, but I did need to understand. The transition, for me, was one of addition, not one of subtraction or denial.

In recent years, when I've been asked, I've tried to be honest about the several parts of that process. Talking about coming home—and *being* home—has allowed me to understand it more fully. In the first place, it has always, powerfully, been a *coming home*: through the confusing days of reentry; bombarded by the dozens of ways in which I had to adjust to a society I knew intimately and yet hardly knew at all; even, or perhaps especially, during the times when I felt most tangibly the threat of deportation.

I came home because this is my land, this New Mexican space of light and openness. For while I was born in New York City, and returned there for four years as a young adult in the late fifties, I was raised in Albuquerque from the age of ten. My parents' choice of this city proved prophetic to my own later needs and choices. These mountains and this desert are my place of physical and emotional regeneration.

I came home because the creative work I feel called upon to do must be done here. I needed to retrieve and feel surrounded by my own language, my culture, and to understand how the places I've lived and the experiences I've had engage that language and culture in my life. In my later forties and early fifties, a bridge-builder still, I wanted to put the pieces of myself together. Conscious of the importance of New York, Spain, Mexico, Cuba Vietnam, Peru, Chile, and Nicaragua, I had to return in order to make sense of the powerful mix that informs my life.

Certain yet uncertain, overwhelmed by change, continually thrown off balance by seemingly insignificant details . . . I remember those first weeks and months. Floyce offered a loving home, and tried hard to cushion the blows. But I couldn't stay inside his apartment forever. I had to emerge, out into a world I claimed. Nevertheless I had little practical idea of how that world really worked.

The therapist I'd seen in Managua had advised me not to take a job for a while. In fact, she said, two years might be needed—for rest and adjustment. But that kind of time is rarely available to those of us who must support ourselves. After a couple of months, I was wondering how I could earn a living—what I might contribute to society, from my long experience in Latin America. And also where I might reasonably expect to be hired with my particular qualifications—or lack of qualifications.

I thought about teaching. I knew I had a lot to share, and I believed college-level students in this country might find my experiences useful. I also sensed that I could learn a lot about my nation's current heartbeat from them: the problems, ideas, and aspirations of a new generation. But would college administrators or department chairs find me hirable? I vividly remember the gestures of friends who put themselves on the line for me, showing me how to write a curriculum vitae, what a syllabus was, what teaching at a university entailed (when I had never graduated from one). I didn't have a formal degree, but I had published more than fifty books. Somewhere, I reasoned, equivalency must be possible.

To make a long story short, I was able to get a job as an adjunct assistant professor at the University of New Mexico, beginning that first September. Women's Studies was a natural home for a woman like myself, who had written more than twenty books of women's oral history. American Studies was also receptive to what I had to offer. Three years later, Trinity College in Hartford, Connecticut, invited me to be a visiting professor in its English department. Since then I have taught at Oberlin College and Macalester College and have plans to return to Trinity and to teach at the University of Delaware. Teaching has become important to me as another kind of bridge-building. But I'm getting ahead of my story.

III THE CASE

Floyce Alexander and I were married in February of 1984, and—as we believed I was a citizen of Mexico—he petitioned for my permanent residency status in March of the same year. I remember the day we went to the Immigration and Naturalization Office in Albuquerque; it's in the old downtown center of the city where I used to walk, filled with a sense of adventure, with my high school girl friends in the early fifties.

We filed the appropriate papers, and one of the officers (Douglas Brown, now CEO of the Albuquerque office) interviewed me briefly. He was casual, interested in "what it was like to live in Cuba and Nicaragua." I understood that those were countries upon which the Reagan administration did not look favorably. And when Brown mentioned that "the FBI would probably be around to ask some questions," I wondered why he couldn't have asked them himself. But there was nothing in the man's initial manner to warn of what would come.

Sixty to ninety days, INS in Albuquerque informed us, was the usual time frame for obtaining a green card, the layperson's description of residency. We were happy to wait. I was beginning to become accustomed to life in a consumer society, as opposed to a society of scarcity. I felt slightly more able to shop at the large department stores, and wasn't as surprised as I'd once been by people's inability to understand where I was coming from much of the time (or my difficulty in transmitting ideas and events outside their immediate life experience). A new love, as well as reunification with my parents, took the sharp edges from this time. An uncle died, and my father generously decided to use the inheritance to build me a house in the foothills next door to his. That was an exciting project, and a stabilizing aspect of the physical process of homecoming.

Sixty days passed, though. Then ninety. Then more than a year. I didn't get my green card. It became clear that mine would not be looked upon as the usual case of a "foreigner" marrying a U.S. citizen and applying for residency. In fact, it was not only my husband whose application for my change in status was approved; the INS also approved applications from my son (who, along with one of my daughters, is a U.S. citizen), and from my mother. But nothing seemed to be happening.

The FBI *didn't* come to our home, but one day in June I was summoned to a taped interview with another INS official. This was our first indication that residency, for me, would not be about family ties or any of the usual questions an applicant is asked. When I entered the room where that interview would take place, I immediately saw a number of my books spread across a large table. They were opened to specific pages, and passages were highlighted in yellow magic marker. I knew then, instantly and powerfully, that my welcome would be pitted against my ideas.

In a friendly, always courteous manner, this new inspector collected further information about my life in Latin America. He seemed most interested in the opinions—my own and those of others—taken from my books, and frequently asked me to elaborate upon one or another of the passages he'd marked. They seemed quite straightforward to me, but I was glad to explain them further.

I wasn't given a sense of how much longer this might take, but I understood that I had been naïve in presuming I might be granted residency without a struggle. Suddenly, the terms changed; this was a battle, and I knew I needed a lawyer familiar with the politics of what was happening. (At first, believing I was dealing with the simple administrative aspects of immigration, we had hired a lawyer who was, in fact, present at that interview about my writing. But he knew as well as we did that mine was becoming a different kind of case.)

That was when I called my old friend Michael Ratner at the Center for Constitutional Rights in New York City and asked him if he thought the Center would be willing to represent me. He immediately said yes, and from then on I was fortunate to have his counsel as well as that of Michael Maggio and David Cole, the wonderful attorneys who saw us through to victory.

Seventeen months elapsed between our March application and the October 1985 deportation order issued by A. L. Guigni, Immigration and Naturalization's district director in El Paso, Texas. I was beginning to be able to *feel* the nature of the government's anger toward a woman, a writer, who holds, expresses, and defends her opinions—even when they dissent from U.S. foreign-policy positions—concerning the Vietnam War, Central America, and other questions.

I've been asked why I point to my womanhood as a target. I know that a man writing what I've written could just as easily have been subject to the persecution I endured. Many have been, and they need our support. In a patriarchal society, however, a woman standing her ground seems to provoke a greater degree of official rage. Women are supposed to cede, acquiesce, say we're sorry. If we don't, we must be punished—at least according to certain fundamentalist principles which are more and more in vogue. Later I'll talk about the particularly gender-offensive line of questioning used by the government attorneys at the hearing in El Paso. Throughout these years of struggle, in press interviews and on radio and TV talk shows, I have frequently been the target of specific assumptions or attitudes directed at me as a woman.

In spite of the fact that during that first year my contact with INS was scant, and our efforts at getting them to make a decision were futile, my feelings about being made a scapegoat were grounded in reality. Once, two of my lawyers came to Albuquerque and we went down to the local INS office to inquire about my case. Douglas Brown refused to shake hands with any of us. He was visibly angered by our presence, and attended to us outside his office, in the common area where people wait endlessly for all sorts of information or responses to their questions.

When the deportation order finally arrived, it was an eleven-page document, ending with the words: "Her writings go far beyond mere dissent, disagreement with, or criticism of the United States or its policies. . . . Your pending application for adjustment of status is hereby DENIED." The word *denied* was written in capitals, as if to avoid confusion. I was given until the thirtieth of October—twenty-eight days—to pack up and leave my husband, my parents, the land where I grew up and to which I had come home. And I was being refused residency explicitly because of what I had written and published. The First Amendment to the Constitution, which I had been raised to believe was an inalienable right, clearly did not protect me from INS.

I remember taking that letter from the rural mailbox by the road in front of my home. There was a blaze of yellow topping the chamisa, and the air was alive with light: October in these foothills. The Justice Department return address prompted me to open the envelope and read its contents standing out in the midst of all that beauty. As I pondered the deportation order, I was determined to fight, for myself and for others, and to win if I possibly could.

Had I been one of the thousands of ordinary people from other countries, applying for U.S. residency without the benefit of my professional position or legal help, I would have had no alternative but to brutally disrupt my life and the lives of those closest to me; I would have had to pack up and leave. But I was lucky. Michael and David assured me those twenty-eight days limited only those who did not have the opportunity or those who had not taken the decision to struggle. I had the right to appeal and could remain here while I did so. I knew I had support, and was ready to do battle.

IV   THE FEELINGS

I don't want to give the impression that I never suffered "down" times. There were plenty of tears—of sorrow as well as rage. There was the anxiety of not being able to plan a future, secure steady employment, concentrate on my writing. I couldn't visit my children who live outside the country because I would have forfeited my appeal by crossing the border, nor could I greet my three grandchildren as they came into the world. How do I measure the weight gain of compulsive eating, or a variety of physical ills—suddenly poor eyesight, nervous tension, hypothyroidism, among others—that may or may not have been intensified by the harassment? And I didn't *ask* to have to struggle with INS and menopause at the same time.

The news media began their complex dance around my case, retreating during the long waiting periods but moving to center stage every time a motion was made or denied, or some phase of the process began or ended. This made me a public person in a way no one would wish for. Ugly hate mail, threats upon my life (often accompanied by a detailed description of how the writer intended to kill me), sudden encounters with strangers who were encouraged by the atmosphere—which eight years of Reaganism had consolidated—to take my person as a target for their anti-communism or fundamentalist righteousness: Incidents of these kinds became part of the fabric of my life.

I remember almost being pushed off the freeway one afternoon by the occupants of another car who glared and pointed as they maneuvered toward me. Once I was threatened in my University of New Mexico office, and the campus police had to attend to my situation as an ongoing task. Sometimes as I entered a movie theater or restaurant, a stranger would scream obscenities, and others would turn and stare. Radio or TV talk shows were the worst; I tried to prepare myself for their high percentage of callers who assuaged personal frustrations by demanding I "go back where I came from" (!) or, more simply, "die."

It's important to make clear that for every one of these attacks, there were at least forty or fifty supportive encounters. Now that the struggle's over, I would like to be able to speak to every person who went out of his or her way to wish me well, offer a few words of encouragement, or—without knowing me personally—involve themselves in the hard work of this case. If I try to list them all, I know I'll leave out many; but I must at least mention Jane Creighton, Ruth Hubbard, Marty Fleisher, Jane Norling, Trisha Franzen,

14

Liz Kennedy, and Bobbi Prebis. They dedicated large parts of their lives to working for my freedom.

In 1987, a man on the street in Berkeley pushed a twenty-dollar bill into my hand, urging me, "Spend it on yourself . . . we need roses as well as bread." A few months later, an American Indian shaman, standing in front of me in an airport counter line, recognized me from my picture in the papers. He said he was on his way to a pow-wow in Oklahoma, and would pray for me there.

A woman in Arizona wrote a moving letter, folded around a five-dollar check from her social security income. A classroom of fifth graders at the Albuquerque school I had attended as a child made my case their year-long project. From them I received letters, drawings, songs, and a great deal of love. Some of the most gratifying demonstrations of support came from people who made sure I knew they didn't agree with my politics, but strongly supported my right to express my ideas. As I say, there was infinitely more support than harassment. But the constant tension that comes from having to be prepared for harassment palpably changes the daily texture of one's life.

Once the official deportation order was served, my status also became a matter for interpretation. Legally, according to the U.S. system of justice, I had a number of appeals open to me. And while the case was on appeal, obviously I had to continue to support myself. The U.S. Immigration and Naturalization Service apparently disagreed. At different times throughout these three and a half years, it seemed to wield its interpretation in whatever way it could in order to cause me the most distress, to the point of contacting more than one institution that offered me employment. Eventually, it was due to the courage of places like Trinity College in Hartford that I could work at all. They defied the harassment, standing by their commitment to the First Amendment.

INS also offered some interesting interpretations of my person. On a 1988 Albuquerque Public Television special, the same Mr. Brown got red in the face as he called me an "alien anarchist!" Only the seriousness of the situation kept me from laughing at his ET vocabulary.

At first I applied for extended permits to work, which were issued without a problem by the Albuquerque INS office. As a person on appeal with what they call first-category family ties, my requests were more a matter of courtesy than anything else; and they knew that as well as we did. In 1986, though, the immigration law changed, and as soon as it did the INS regional director in El Paso revoked my work permit. Agency lawyers at my subsequent hearing before an Immigration judge were quick to point out that I continued to teach without permission. The judge gave this charge only "one scintilla of importance." I now want to talk about that immigration hearing in some detail, because it was there, I believe, that we all came to understand the government's hard-line position in my case.

V THE HEARING

The law under which aliens may be excluded or deported from the United States is the McCarran-Walter Immigration and Nationality Act of 1952. President Truman vetoed the act, but a McCarthyite Congress overrode his objections. With some modifications, McCarran-Walter continues to govern immigration today. One of its thirty-three parts, known by laypersons as "the ideological exclusion clause," makes it possible to deny entry to those whose writing or speaking "advocates the international, economic, or governmental doctrines of world communism."

That's the way the statute reads, and it is obvious there may be as many interpretations of what those words actually mean as there are officials with the power to interpret them. In fact, this is *very much* a matter of interpretation: What does advocating the doctrines of world communism really mean, where does freedom of expression come in, and *who* has the ability or right to do the interpreting? Can we expect intelligent literary criticism from a middle-level INS official? Or even a rational interpretation of political and historical texts?

And that's what those four days in an El Paso courtroom were all about. Judge Martin Spiegel heard evidence from both sides. We brought witnesses who attested to my family ties and contributions to the community. We brought witnesses who were granted expert status by the court, who spoke of my literary work, my photography, my teaching; who addressed the political and literary language used in the sixties and seventies, as well as realities of life in Cuba and Nicaragua. My daughter testified, as did my parents and husband. The courtroom was packed with friends and colleagues from the University of New Mexico, students of mine, women from the feminist communities of Albuquerque and Las Cruces, old union organizers from the Salt of the Earth miners' strike in Silver City, and farm workers from the border area.

The prosecution produced no human witnesses at all. What

chief lawyer for INS Guadalupe Gonzalez presented to the court was my work and my work alone—2,270-plus pages of it! Some of the poems or articles, originally written by me in English, had been translated by hurried or quasi-literate INS translators from published Spanish into a crude English I could neither recognize nor acknowledge. At one point the Service prepared to show what they termed "anti-American cartoons" published in the magazine I edited in Mexico. The judge said he didn't think that was necessary.

Those four days of testimony are available in a court transcript numbering close to a thousand pages. It's difficult to choose examples from the many I might quote. But I want to continue to talk about freedom of expression and dissent, and what that freedom really means: how it is frequently betrayed and how it may translate—subtly or blatantly—into censorship or self-censorship, deeply affecting a person's capacity for thought and action. So I'll stick to the line of questioning that most clearly addressed those issues.

After doing her best to define me as a wanton degenerate (some of her questions included asking me if it was true that I had posed nude for art classes in the fifties in New York and waitressed in a gay bar there in the same decade, and why several of my children had different fathers), Guadalupe Gonzalez asked me what it had been like to "publish in a magazine that also published Communists." She pointed out that one issue of *El Corno Emplumado* had been dedicated to Black Panther leader Huey Newton, that a poem of mine was titled "Che," and that Marxist material had been advertised in a bookstore ad in our magazine.

Judge Spiegel wouldn't let me respond when Gonzalez asked if "I would take up arms to defend the United States against Castro-Communist Cuba," reminding her that conscientious objection exists here for citizens and therefore certainly for aliens. But he did let her ask if I had ever written a poem in praise of free enterprise. When she questioned my 1960s spelling of America with a *k*, sometimes even with three *k*'s, and I replied that it was a metaphor, she did not understand what that meant.

If it hadn't been clear from the beginning, the hearing in El Paso solidly established mine as a First Amendment case. It was all about what I had written, my opinions which differed from those of a series of U.S. administrations over issues ranging from racism and sexism at home to foreign policy in Southeast Asia, Cuba, and Central America. Sometimes there didn't seem to be enough in my own writings to damn me as conclusively as the INS lawyers would have wished, so they introduced as evidence things written about me by others.

Of course, many of my opinions, particularly those about U.S. policy in Vietnam, were shared by hundreds of thousands of others in this country. But they were citizens, the government said; they were free to think or say whatever they wished. I had "renounced" my citizenship (this was the word they used, echoed over and over in the press); they claimed that it had been a political rather than an economic act, and that as a consequence I should be denied freedom of expression or the right to reside in the land of my birth.

The line of questioning during those four days also made clear just how dangerously close to McCarthy-era assumptions the Reagan administration brought this country. Anticommunism was the underlying tenet of the INS position, as expressed by its spokespeople, its lawyers, its officials and even its judges. Judge Spiegel did not challenge INS language with regard to the characterization of places and people; he reflected similar biases in the opinion he eventually rendered. During the hearing it was always "Castro-Communist Cuba" or "the totalitarian government of Nicaragua," rather than simply Cuba or Nicaragua.

The government lawyers literally went so far as to equate U.S. presidential utterance with papal infallibility; David Cole describes this as the "novel doctrine of conclusive and binding 'Presidential Facts.' " In an article in *The National Law Journal*, ("The 1952 McCarren-Walter Act: Is It Irrelevant in Today's World?" Monday, May 29, 1989) Cole wrote that the INS attorneys acted as though administration political claims cannot be questioned in a court of law: "It is a 'Presidential Fact,' for example, that the Sandinista Front is an evil force of communism, because the president says it is. It therefore follows that Randall, who has dared to write positively of the Sandinistas, should be excluded from this country for 'advocating the doctrines of world communism.' . . . According to the INS brief," Cole explained, "the American nation [presumably through the voice of Ronald Reagan] has decided communism is 'bad' and capitalism is 'good,' and anyone who fails to toe that line should not be permitted to live among us."

We made a brilliant showing in El Paso. Some of my witnesses, like Adrienne Rich, Nelson Valdes, my mother, my daughter, and others, were eloquent. The government's testimony was based on a flimsy portrayal of guilt by association, and its 1950s tone and implications alternated between the frightening and the absurd. But we were yet to discover just how close to fifties thought and action the eighties had become.

18

VI IMMIGRATION LAW

Before the year was out, Judge Spiegel upheld the district director's deportation order. His thirty-two-page decision was most interesting, though, in how it differed from Guigni's. While Guigni hadn't actually found me ineligible under McCarran-Walter *but had based the order upon his discretionary powers to exclude me*, Spiegel said that in his *discretion* he would have granted me the right to stay, because of family ties and service to the community. He *did*, however, find me ineligible under McCarran-Walter.

Both men claimed to have read my work, but they came to opposite conclusions about its bearing on my eligibility for U.S. residency. Freedom of expression, protected by the First Amendment, should render the ideological exclusion clause of McCarran-Walter unconstitutional. However, it was becoming clearer that immigration law in this country is used as a political weapon in the hands of people unfamiliar with the literary nature of language and incompetent to agree about the definition of the relevant statute.

Had I been less naïve about INS and its self-conceived independent status vis-à-vis U.S. constitutional guarantees, I might not have been so surprised. In the same *National Law Journal* article, David Cole points out that "in more than two hundred years, the U.S. Supreme Court has never held an immigration law unconstitutional," and "at least since the turn of this century, U.S. immigration law has authorized the deportation and exclusion of aliens for their political beliefs and associations. . . . Aliens can be deported or excluded for uttering statements, admitting beliefs or joining organizations that would be constitutionally protected if uttered, admitted or joined by a U.S. citizen." Xenophobia, racism, and in my case sexism, are tools with which popular support has been garnered for this type of truly un-American activity.

El Paso is history, and I won't go into detail about the way this case began wending its way through the system. We (Norman Mailer, Arthur Miller, Toni Morrison, Anne Noggle, Grace Paley, PEN American Center, Rose Styron, William Styron, Helene Vann, Kurt Vonnegut, Alice Walker, Dr. Mary Martha Weigle and I) launched a countersuit, which didn't fare well in Washington district court. Later, the Supreme Court refused to hear it.

Meanwhile, the deportation case proceeded to the next level: the Board of Immigration Appeals (BIA) in Washington, D.C. It was heard before that five-member board, with fifteen minutes allotted to the attorneys for each side, in October 1987. Guadalupe Gonzalez traveled from El Paso to argue for the INS. But here she went further than she had in Judge Spiegel's courtroom. Rather than cite from cases or points of law relevant to the government's position, she simply quoted from Allan Bloom's *The Closing of the American Mind*. "The danger is that we will dilute the battle between freedom and communism to the level of no-fault auto insurance," she told the Board. "The danger is that we will view this case in a context where there is no right or wrong. But there is a right and a wrong. The American Congress has stated that our system of government is right, and it is good, and the Communist system is bad. We *are* an intolerant government. We are intolerant of world communism, and we are intolerant of those individuals like Randall, who attempt to increase its hold on the world. . . ."

There's really no clearer example than this of the government's point of view on this issue, at least the point of view of those within our government—the zealots—who would reduce complex social and political thought to the simplicity of fundamentalist gibberish. The Board of Immigration Appeals heard the oral arguments and then sat on my case for more than a year and a half—through the passage of the 1988 Senate Foreign Relations Authorization Act that did away with some of McCarran-Walter's worst features, as well as a reversal, one year later, of the part of that act which favored my situation. When the BIA finally ruled, it was a surprise to us all. But more about that later.

A number of congresspeople, over the past several years and during the time while the BIA was deliberating my case, have attempted to pass legislation designed to modernize important aspects of McCarran-Walter. Barney Frank (D.-Mass.) has been one of the most ardent proponents of a more rational immigration law, and Alan Simpson (R.-Wyo.) has proposed modifications that also address some of that law's most antiquated clauses. It is clear that we need to keep fighting for the repeal of McCarran-Walter. There is no reason that a country that holds itself up as a model of democratic principles should deny entry to people like Pablo Neruda, Gabriel García Marquez, Carlos Fuentes, Farley Mowat, Hortensia Allende—and deny the American people access to their presence.

Back, though, to the particulars of my case. As the summer of 1989 began, almost four years had passed since the district director's deportation order (more than five years since I returned to the United States), and the case still hadn't made its way into the federal court system. Now that it's over, I think it's important to explore the issues of free expression, dissent, censorship, self-censorship, harassment, and innuendo as they played themselves out in my life. So what I want to talk about here is what it *felt* like to take on this kind of battle; how it changed the nature of my thought, work, interaction with others, relationships, energy, confrontation, sense of self; how it affected my body, my mind, my individual and collective memory, my consciousness.

VII THE HIDDEN THREATS

Before exploring what it's meant in my life to have my freedom of expression threatened, it might be useful to define the basic concept of expression. Expression is the externalization of thought and feeling. It is the exposure to others of that thought and feeling, and in the process, ours and theirs interact to form the bridge across which the human condition itself must pass if it is to live and grow in all its disparate complexity.

Forcible opposition to expression, or its denial, constitutes repression. We have come to identify repression with acts of foreign totalitarian dictatorships, or with police brutality against the unarmed community of our own inner-city neighborhoods. Repression is most often directed against a particular group—the poor or homeless, people of color, gays and lesbians, people with AIDS—by a state that fears their struggle for justice; or by the authoritarian head of a family (usually male) against the women and children he batters in an attempt to alleviate what he may perceive as the system's battering of him.

But the repressive act always begins with the repression of an idea, be it one of freedom or justice or simply the recognition of difference. With particular attention to expression and its repression as concerns the writer of books, Kurt Vonnegut offered some insightful testimony before the International Economic Policy Subcommittee of the Senate Foreign Relations Committee in August of 1986. Speaking for the 2,000 members of the American writers and editors organization PEN, Vonnegut said:

> Precisely because we are writers, we know that reading one another's books does not replicate face-to-face confrontation. That is, as readers of foreign literature, we respond with particular commitment to the truth of expression inherent to all literatures; as writers, we are acutely aware of the social and cultural contexts that are lost in translation. But when we meet, the insistent articulation of these *dialogues* fuses those perceptions and experiences we have in common, and this fusion in turn yields a common perspective from

which we begin to comprehend the other's differences and singularities. Such exchanges might have once been deemed the luxuries of the intellect. Today, in a world overwhelmed by internationalism, they are morally imperative.

Vonnegut told the committee that "PEN International—the only worldwide association of literary writers—has survived, and thrived, throughout its sixty-five years of existence for one reason: Its members, who together represent the sweep of cultural histories and political systems that define the world today, have met and continue to meet annually at conferences and congresses held in different countries." He went on to reproach Congress with the irony implicit in the fact that "when America's turn came to host a PEN congress in January of 1986, there was doubt and consternation as to whether such a meeting of PEN could take place in the United States, in one of the leading democracies in the world and the only one with a First Amendment. PEN members from everywhere in the world," he said, "had been welcomed to meet in far less free countries, such as Yugoslavia."

The U.S. Immigration and Naturalization Service's deportation order against me threatened my sense of identity every day from October 2, 1985, to the day of our victory in August of 1989. The message was clear: If I did not relinquish my ideas, and my right to express them, I risked losing my home, in the profound definition of that word: history, memory, place, family, cultural context, personal process, and ability to function.

But if I gave up, if I said I was sorry and wouldn't write those things again—something they seem intent upon forcing women, particularly, to do—if I accepted their patriarchal *punishment*, lowered my voice and turned against the truth of my struggle, I would lose much more. I would lose the very *meaning* of that truth, for myself and for all those who believe my freedom of expression is linked to theirs.

These are big words and concepts. They tend to become rhetorical or even meaningless if divorced from the daily examples of what this can mean. Throughout these four and a half years, every time I stood before a lectern I wondered who the INS agents in the audience were. (On several occasions they themselves announced their presence: In Buffalo the local head of INS attended one of my lectures; in Minneapolis two men who showed up at a fund raiser identified themselves as working for the Service.)

While teaching, I was always conscious of the possibility that Accuracy in Academia, the ultra-conservative bulldog group dedicated to attacking dissent on campuses, might have student spies in my classes. It was important to me not to allow the shadow of these presences to change what I wanted to say. I literally and consciously recommitted myself daily to that determination.

I often wondered who I was in the eyes of my students. The vast majority of them were born when the McCarthy era was history. We know how quickly history itself becomes distorted or even erased completely in today's educational system. What was happening to me—someone who had been served a deportation order because of what she wrote—was almost impossible for many of my students to comprehend. Besides, they had come to know me; I didn't *seem* like a threat to national security. Over and over again, they told me they couldn't understand it.

It was a delicate balance, in this respect, between keeping news reporters and television camera crews out of my classrooms while at the same time being willing to talk about the case and use it as an educational tool through which my students might understand what's possible, even in a democracy, when constitutional principles are undermined or ignored. I want to say that, throughout my three years of teaching while under order of deportation, my students were wonderfully and movingly supportive. Some of them came to El Paso. They worked on my defense committees, launched educational or fund-raising events, passed support motions through student governing bodies; and, with the victory, congratulations have come from supporters whose names I barely remember.

One of the most satisfying incidents with a student goes back to my days at the University of New Mexico. She remained silent in class through the first month at least. When I questioned her lack of participation, she said she was nervous about giving her opinions because she didn't agree with my politics, or with those expressed by most of her classmates. "I'm a Republican," she told me, "I voted for Ronald Reagan. And I don't think that would go over very well in here."

I used that student's concerns to reiterate my belief that all opinions are important, and in my courses all opinions are respected. Months later, just before the El Paso hearing, this young woman was willing to testify to the court that studying with me she had never felt disrespected in her beliefs or coerced into changing them. She, like all my students I hope, found my classroom a place in which the most important process was that of *learning to think*, not learning to mimic the professor's ideas or anyone's else's.

VIII TO KEEP DOING THE WORK

I wrote and published six books between the date of the deportation order and the end of the case. I also completed one novel and part of another, which are still unpublished. Every written word carried with it the double-edged question: If I say this, will it make things worse? But how could I not?

One book became a battlefield upon which these questions played themselves out in a particularly painful way. It's called *This Is About Incest* and is a collection of poetry, prose, and photographs detailing my personal struggle to come to terms with the reclaimed memory of my grandfather's incest in my life.

The struggle itself was interesting, in the context of the case. I didn't *ask* for abuse memories to surface; no one does. But when they did—in the office of a wonderful therapist who made a great difference in my life throughout these difficult years—I took them on as I've accepted other challenges: with the full power of my creative capabilities.

A phobia and an eating disorder marked the way back to the memories I needed to reclaim. I remember experiencing my first body memory signaling the incest itself just days before we had to pack up our lives and go to the immigration hearing in El Paso. My therapist packed up her practice as well, being one of a large group of supporters and friends who accompanied me on that part of the journey. The case was the priority then; other work would just have to wait.

A month or so after the hearing, I was able to resume the incest work. As an artist, as someone whose natural tendency is to resolve problems through the creativity of writing and photography, I found myself searching for images, hunting down old family portraits and letters, looking at eyes and hands in new ways. I found myself writing out the discovery and the anguish, turning the reclaimed memory into something I believed would be useful in my own healing and as an offering to others going through the same unraveling of secrets the patriarchy protects.

And so that little book was born. But if the writing of it was the logical product of my process of abuse discovery, it wasn't an easy book to publish. There were other people's feelings to consider; why I had to put it all out there for everyone to see was a question several in my immediate family asked. In time, most of those close to me have come around; different levels of struggle, and in some cases memories of their own, have made it possible for them to understand and even support my decision.

In a more public sense, *This Is About Incest* found a place for itself that continues to tell me it was an important risk to take, an important statement to make. Letters have come to me from all over the country, from readers who have been helped in their own struggles by my revelation of the process. When I read the poems, to small groups of women or before larger mixed audiences, there are always dozens of survivors who tell me they're glad the poems are part of our collective history.

Taking the risk implicit in making public my experience with incest taught me a great deal. On a personal level, it enabled me to think about and recognize abuse in the lives of my own children; and it opened the possibility of their dealing with these issues in whatever ways their particular processes demand. In a larger sense, and because I don't separate what some people refer to as personal from political issues, my struggle with incest has provided some insights into my struggle for the freedom to dissent. In both cases I had to protect and nurture my integrity against covert or overt pressures from an authority that preferred my silence, promising rewards if I would only *be good*, punishment if I wasn't. In both cases I learned that my integrity was the only thing they absolutely *could not take from me*.

But there's another area in which I *wasn't* able to externalize the full dimension of my beliefs, in which I couldn't risk speaking out. About a year into the fight, my personal evolution was taking me to a recognition of my identity as a lesbian. The public assumption of sexual or affectational preference is difficult for many in this country, who simply choose not to take on that battle in our heterosexist and homophobic society. Increasingly, many gays and lesbians *are* taking it on, because they believe that coming out ultimately makes it easier for our children as well as ourselves. Given the consistency with which I've spoken out in my life, my emotional tendency was towards the latter option. My immigration case, however, restricted that choice.

Among McCarran-Walter's thirty-three clauses, there is one that makes "sexual deviancy" grounds for excludability or deportation. That is this particular law's euphemism for homosexuality. Privately, I opened my arms to my lesbian identity and the extraordinary relief and community it brought with it. Close to three years ago now, I began living with the woman who is my life partner. Together we were forced to deal with the public limitations of our life in the context of my case.

It was clear to us that homosexuality is no more constitutional a ground for deportation than is the expression of so-called subversive ideas or association with a variety of progressive organizations. It will be important to fight the battle for freedom of sexual preference. But that wasn't a fight to which I could commit myself in the context of this case, and introducing this new element would undoubtedly have complicated the process enormously. My lawyers wanted me, if possible, not to be explicit about my lesbian identity. If it came out, so to speak, we would deal with it; and I want to acknowledge their willingness to take it on if it came to that. Our feeling was that raising this issue would have detracted from the important First Amendment question, however, and so I agreed to try to keep it under wraps.

What did this mean, though, in terms of daily life? At what personal cost was I forced to keep this "secret"? Obviously, my partner and I suffer the oppression of all lesbians and gay men in a heterosexist society. But in our case there was always that extra burden, pressured as we were by the rigors of the case, unable to publicly express our caring, as release or panacea. Hundreds of thousands of lesbians and gay men in this country cannot come out for fear of losing jobs, children, support of family or friends. For us, there was the additional threat of instantly losing my case— which meant struggle, choice, place. My parents as well as children were solidly and lovingly with us from the beginning. And the lesbian community proved sensitive to our need for discretion.

For my partner, this situation brought a particular brand of invisibility which was often painful to endure. Her courage and commitment contributed enormously to keeping us both on track. For me, perhaps the most difficult aspect of my inability to be fully who I am was the fact that I could not write out of my lesbian sensibility. This meant not just the obvious restriction on a love poem or in a review of another's work, but a barrier to deep, engaged honesty that is possible only when one is able to write from every part of one's identity.

This was particularly difficult in the process of producing Ruth Hubbard's and my book, *The Shape of Red: Insider/Outsider Reflections*. It's a volume of letters in which the two of us, as women and friends, discuss everything from politics and work to sexuality and motherhood. I agonized over the final publishable form of one of my letters, and almost decided to give up on discussing my sexuality at all. Ruth was thoughtful and patient; she urged me to walk right up to the edge, exposing what I could and leaving the rest to the reader's imagination. As always, when faced with choices about how much to risk, I'm grateful for the vision and support of someone like Ruth, who believes as I do that risk itself most often points towards freedom.

Just as the repression of ideas evokes resistance, this limitation on my writing, because I couldn't express my whole identity, also resulted in some not altogether negative by-products. One day, when I complained bitterly that I wasn't doing the writing I needed to be doing, one of my lawyers said, "Why don't you write a novel?" My son also encouraged me in that, and the almost finished two novels I've been able to produce since then might not have happened were it not for my need to express ideas and feelings I couldn't deal with in the first person.

As with other areas of this struggle, though, there are things the government took from me that are lost forever. One is the experience of joining 600,000 lesbians, gay men, and others for the great march on Washington in October of 1988. We could have gone, of course; in retrospect I'm sure it wouldn't have meant anything in terms of the case. But several years of media coverage had accustomed me to being picked out in a crowd. I played it safe. It was one of a number of times in which censorship became self-censorship: the worst kind.

In close emotional association with issues like incest, and even with a particular sexual identification—if the society in which you function constantly holds them up to negative scrutiny—is the problem of *shame*. Women, especially, are conditioned to feel shame almost as a matter of course and in a wide range of situations. I wasn't vulnerable to shame as a lesbian (perhaps I was too old for that). Neither was it a significant part of dealing with the incest (enough others had spoken out before me to create a community in which I could feel supported). But shame did have its place in the feelings generated by this case.

When the anxiety over the possibility of losing their daughter was stark on my parents' face, I told them, "I'm sorry." When I had to ask for help from friends who were already overburdened with multiple issues in their own lives, I'd hear myself prefacing a request with the words, "I'm really sorry but. . . ." It was hard to sustain the knowledge that this *wasn't my fault*. The government had launched this battle, not I. Yet how quickly and easily I assumed the blame!

A wonderful muralist, single mother and close friend, Jane Norling, organized early on the Northern California Friends of Margaret Randall. It remained one of the most active of more than twenty defense committees across the country, at one time even assuming tasks of nationwide coordination. I remember Jane, overburdened and harried, telling me a couple of years into the struggle, "If it hadn't been you, I never would have taken this on!" And after it was all over and I was talking about how badly I felt about the time and energy so many had expended on my behalf, Jane again was the one who cut me short: "We didn't do this just because a woman somewhere was being deported. We did it because of what you've given us, your books . . . they're important to so many people."

When sticking to one's principles seems to produce nothing more than rage, exhaustion, and ongoing depression, when it would seem so much easier to cede just a bit, to imply a change of voice or heart, it's important to remember what's at stake. Integrity and dignity are qualities that can be taken from a person only in extreme situations of isolation and torture, and sometimes not even then. In my situation they would have to have been willingly forfeited. And integrity and dignity become enormously important in a struggle of an individual against a system. You come to realize that, yes, political repression *can* separate you from family, from place, from many of the choices you have made. But it cannot strip you of your core identity; it *cannot* diminish your dignity. In fact, it strengthens both and makes them easier and easier to hold onto.

IX THE SUPPORT

When I say an individual against a system, I'm not saying I was alone in my struggle. Far from it. Thousands—family and friends but also people I've never met—came with me every bit of the way. And many of the ideas and activities that informed my fight against deportation are themselves extraordinary examples of creative expression and activism.

The Center for Constitutional Rights estimates that it cost us a quarter of a million dollars to fight this case. And that doesn't include what we've been charged as taxpayers so the government could wage its side of the battle. The money came as donations from direct mailing, button and poster campaigns, house parties, raffles, auctions, media coverage, and many original efforts on the part of hundreds of people who gave up pieces of their lives to work on committees or involve themselves in other ways.

Audre Lorde, Adrienne Rich, Sonia Sanchez, Robert Creeley, Diane di Prima, Floyce Alexander, Luci Tapahonso, Joy Harjo, Gene Frumkin, Larry Goodell, Dennis Brutus, John Nichols, Ron Kovic, Alice Walker, Omar Cabezas, Manlio Argueta, Denise Levertov, Susan Sherman, Howard Zinn, Merle Woo, Harold Jaffee, and many others read or spoke for the case. Holly Near, John Boccino, Casselberry-DuPreé, Marta Hogan, Linda Collier, and others played and sang for it. Crowsfeet, The Dance Brigade, Streetwise, and other groups danced for it.

The great (and, sadly, recently deceased) painter Elaine de Kooning made an old portrait she'd done of me into a beautiful full-color poster, which was then sold to benefit the cause. It was Helene Vann who made the first "Keep Randall—Deport McCarran-Walter" button; later Jane Norling added a beautiful design to a reissued version. In Seattle the Red and Black Book Collective organized a Bowl-a-thon for Free Speech, complete with special T-shirts.

David Wilk, of Long River Books in Connecticut, printed a pamphlet of my coming home poems; the proceeds from sales, including his percentage, were donated to my defense fund. Master printer Kathy Kuehn produced an elegant broadside from a short poem of mine, with specially stamped envelopes, a thousand of which were sold to raise money. Peter Stambler, in Wisconsin, organized a marathon fund-raising reading of my work. The Syracuse Cultural Workers Collective dedicated the page for May in their 1989 Peace Calendar to a collage representation of my fight. These are only a few of the great number of offerings, activities and events that kept the issues alive and some money coming in.

At Trinity College in Hartford, 165 faculty, administrators, and staff members signed a petition urging immediate granting of my residency. Berkeley, California, proclaimed February 2, 1986, Margaret Randall Day in their city, and Cambridge, Massachusetts, distinguished me with a certificate—surely not because either had any previous knowledge of me, but because they deem freedom of expression essential to this country's way of life. Unions, religious orders and councils, professional organizations and conferences unanimously raised their voices against the affront to freedom of expression and dissent symbolized by the deportation order against me. All these, and many more, are examples of communities of people confronting official censorship with creative struggle.

X FAMILY

I hope this conveys something of the texture of these years. As the case moved from defeat to defeat, I continued to write, make pictures, teach, love, mother, bake bread, and breathe, in the rocky, juniper-dotted foothill country surrounding me in the home I hoped I would not have to leave. My partner hoped this too, as she adjusted the daily contours of her life to the demands of the struggle. My parents—now 79 and 83—also hoped. Their little adobe house sits between ours and the mountain face. It had taken me almost three decades to come home; my mother and father did everything in their power to help make sure I could stay.

Everything in their power . . . thinking back, from this place of having won, I imagine it may have been my parents who felt most powerless through these years of struggle. My mother worried each time a news report reprinted a lie about her daughter. I'm still not sure if this experience managed to teach her—against a lifelong barrage of media conditioning—not to believe it "just 'cuz it says so in the paper." She spent hundreds of hours, over these years, urging people to write letters on my behalf. She was the one who carefully kept the scrapbooks: a record of every brief, opinion, affidavit, affirmation, article, poster, flyer.

Early on, she also had an experience that probably helped to keep her going in the context of such continuous pressure: Sitting in the car one day, waiting for my father to return from an errand, she told herself that if he was the twentieth person to emerge from the door he'd entered, we would be victorious. And she started counting. As time went by, when we were most depressed she often reminded us that he had indeed been the twentieth person. When we won, she reminded us again.

One of only two times I cried during the hearing in El Paso was when my mother was on the stand. She is a small woman, almost so thin as to appear frail. But she rose to enormous heights of energy and righteous indignation when one of my attorneys asked if she had anything further she wished to address to the court. It was 1986, and she spoke about the nation's anniversary, about the Statue of Liberty and what it could mean if freedom of expression was not only honored but guaranteed. It was an extraordinary moment, one that I don't believe many in that room will forget.

My father was a rock of support in his constant, quiet way. I know that he sent every spare penny to CCR; again and again, when xeroxed sheets of donation checks would come for me to respond to with the letters I always wrote to everyone who gave, I would see a copy of a check from him. But the greatest strength I got from my father was the fact that he never wavered in his pride. I felt that he was proud of the stand I took, and wouldn't have wanted me to back down—even if it eventually meant another (and certainly final) painful separation.

When I think about where my stubborn attachment to honesty

comes from, I know I owe that to my father. "It's just not right," I remember his tone of voice throughout my childhood and growing up years. He'd be talking about some injustice, someone who had been wronged, however small the offense. Throughout my struggle with immigration, my father held to his belief that justice would prevail. A great example of that belief is the house he built for me, next door to his own.

My children were always with me, from the several countries where they make their homes. They rallied support and tried to keep up with each new turn of events. It must have been hard for them, as their mother went through this, to be so far away. They were raised on struggle, and in places where it has been particularly raw at times, so they understood the forces at play. But that probably didn't make it any easier for them when I sometimes expressed my anxiety in letters or on the phone.

My son and his wife live in Paris with their two small children. My oldest daughter lived in Cuba for most of these years; communication with her was difficult because of the fragmented relations between the two countries. Now she's in Mexico, and we can reach one another more easily by phone, while my next daughter—also in Mexico—has recently moved to an apartment without a phone. There have been a number of times during these years when I could not travel that I felt an intense need to be with my children: after the terrible 1987 earthquake in Mexico City, or when they've suffered more personal problems of their own. We've managed one large reunion here in Albuquerque as well as other more partial get-togethers, but I've yet to see any of those who live outside this country in their own space.

My youngest daughter, Ana, has been in the United States since my struggle with INS began. We are on opposite sides of the country now, but visit frequently; the problems of contact haven't been the same as with the others. Three years back she was living with me, and I remember her coming home from a waitressing job one day and talking about a co-worker who'd asked, "Aren't you the one whose mother is a Commie?" So that kind of harassment hasn't been totally absent from my children's lives either. Ana was also on the stand at the El Paso hearing; hers was the second testimony that brought tears to my eyes. It was simply about seeing her there, seventeen years old and participating with such dignity.

If I had to isolate the single most difficult thing about this case in terms of family, I'd say it was not being able to be with *my* children when they had *theirs*. As a former midwife, as well as a mother, that was a dream I had nurtured. It became one of the irretrievable things the U.S. Immigration and Naturalization Service took from my life. In October 1987, my first grandchild, Lia Margarita, was born in Paris. Luis Rodrigo followed in Mexico City in February of 1988. And Martin came along in August of 1989, again in Paris, just weeks before our victory.

XI VICTORY

And what about the victory? It came, sudden and unexpected—at least in its origin and form—in the last days of July 1989. I was working on my new novel, sitting before the word processor by my studio window with its dramatic view of the Sandia Mountains. The telephone rang; it was Michael Maggio's office. "Is this Margaret Randall?" a secretary's voice asked. "Michael wants to speak with you; it's important."

Needless to say, my heart tried to push its way up into the back of my throat. An urgent message: in my mind, battered by a long series of defeats, it could only be a threatening one. At the same time, I knew the case was long overdue for a ruling by the Board of Immigration Appeals. If this was news of that Board's negative decision, well, that was what we expected.

Then I heard Michael telling me we'd won!

The BIA was the last decision-making body within the administrative INS courts. Its chairman, David L. Milhollan, wrote the favorable decision to which two of the other members subscribed. They found that I had become a Mexican motivated by economic duress, and therefore had not lost my U.S. citizenship. All other issues then became irrelevant. It was a 3–2 ruling, with Board member Fred W. Vacca writing a scathing dissenting opinion, more or less a rehash of the Guadalupe Gonzalez argument.

The decision could not be appealed to the courts, and the media immediately wrote the victory as final. I was numb. While the phone rang incessantly, the house filled with flowers, telegrams, and friends with champagne and balloons, I tried to imagine what life would be like, now that I could get on with it. Now that I could hold my grandchildren, tell my partner I loved her—even on our telephone which I must presume is tapped—maybe even get a real job.

But my mind kept telling my body: Don't let go, not yet. And my mind was right. Before twenty-four hours had passed, news came that the INS lawyers had requested a thirty-day stay, in order to ask the attorney general to reverse the decision. We spent close to another month, like human yo-yos, trying once again to bury the emotion and wait. This was a particularly difficult period. Most of the media ran only the initial story; details of complications aren't the kind of thing that makes the news. So strangers would come up to me in the street and tell me how glad they were that things had "worked out." I never knew whether to launch into an explanation of what was actually happening or just say, "Thank you very much."

Finally, toward the end of August, the Service "determined that it (would) not file a motion for reconsideration of the Board's decision." Apparently they felt it was time to give up. Victory, filtered as it had been through stops and starts, was ours. Eventually, the flowers that arrived in the wake of the absolute win were indistinguishable from those that had brightened our home after the first news. As I write this, several weeks later, the house remains filled with all their joyous colors.

In recognizing my U.S. citizenship, the BIA gave me a full personal victory. Politically, the outcome may seem less clear. The citizenship decision mutes the First Amendment considerations, and that's good for an administration in which many conservatives are fighting against immigration reform; especially as legislation modifying McCarran-Walter once again comes before Congress. But I believe the central issues of freedom of expression and freedom of dissent have not been lost.

Longtime New Mexico political activist Dorothy Cline, one among many from whom I've had messages, wrote that "the system worked but the wheels were rusty, out of date and had to be repaired. But *not* replaced—McCarran-Walter is still with us. Certainly the case . . . must have helped to influence opinion. When it is repealed, you can take a good share of the credit."

I would agree that we fought an important struggle, one that many within the administration were anxious to silence. We educated tens of thousands of people in this country about the nature of U.S. immigration law and about threats to our freedoms which affect us all. We need to keep on fighting until all the laws that govern who may or may not come into our country are brought into line with constitutional principles.

The pragmatists within the administration wanted to see an end to this case. It's interesting that the three Board members who subscribed to the favorable ruling were Nixon and Ford appointees; the two who signed the dissenting opinion were appointed by Ronald Reagan. They and many others are the zealots of these years: the Eliot Abramses, Ollie Norths, Jerry Falwells, the names and faces we will continue to see on the other side of the barricades in our battles for human dignity, for just immigration laws, against racism and intervention, and for reproductive choice.

The zealots may call themselves "pro-life," but in most of today's battles they come up on the side of death. The pragmatists in many instances may also hold conservative points of view, but they understand that keeping faith with democratic principles can often be important to the maintenance of capitalism. Some also hold constitutional values they don't want to see destroyed.

These are times when victories are scarce. As the reality of this one sinks in, I begin to feel a lightening, a renewal of energy I know I'll need for the other battles we face. Coming home must bring peace, but never complacency. I don't want to forget a single instance of pain or frustration, and I want to be able to place my anger where it belongs, squarely in the laps of those who from positions of abusive power would punish, stigmatize, harass, and persecute. But I want also to remember the lessons: how people come together, what creativity is born in struggle, what faith is held in it. As I continue to build my bridges and walk across them, I am filled with the vision of the hands waving behind me and those reaching out to welcome me to the other side.

—Albuquerque, New Mexico
Summer, 1989

Jemez ruins, northern New Mexico, 1989.

Monument Valley, Four Corners area, Utah, 1989.

Rio Grande, northern New Mexico, 1988.

The great saguaros, outside of Tucson, 1989.

Margaret Randall at National Women's Studies Association, Atlanta, summer 1987. Photo: Marilyn Humphries.

Margaret Randall at one of the plenaries, National Women's Studies Association, Atlanta, summer 1987. Photo: Marilyn Humphries.

Margaret Randall and daughter Ana, El Paso Courthouse, March 1986. Photo: Jack Levine.

Salvadoran writer Manlio Argueta and Margaret Randall at fundraiser, NYC, 1986. Photo: Mel Rosenthal.

Margaret Randall and her mother Elinor Randall, at home in Albuquerque, 1988. Photo: Colleen McKay.

Ana, Gregory, Ximena, and Sarah at the Albuquerque reunion, August
1988. Photo: Jack Levine.

Barbara Byers, 1989.

IMMIGRATION LAW

When I ask the experts
"How much time do I have?"
I don't want an answer in years
or arguments.

I must know if there are hours enough
to mend this relationship,
see a book all the way to its birthing,
stand beside my father
on his journey.

I want to know how many seasons of chamisa
will be yellow then grey-green
and yellow
                    /light/
                              again,
how many red cactus flowers
will bloom beside my door.

I do not want to follow language
like a dog with its tail between its legs.

I need time equated with music,
hours rising in bread,
years deep from connections.

The present always holds a tremor of the past.

Give me a handful of future
to rub against my lips.

October, 1985

TALK TO ME

Talk to me. Three
words
moving with heavy feet
across the open spaces.

A signal,
or the beginning of a poem.

Talk to me. Not meaning
"How are things going?" Not meaning
"They *can't* do this to you"
(they can, they are)
not even
"What can I do to help?"

Do it, that's all.
Please.
No more questions, no more
knowledgeable statements.

Three words. Begin a poem. Take your life
and use it.

Winter, 1986

UNDER ATTACK

for Marian McDonald

Listen. These voices are under attack.

Ismaela of the dark tobacco house. Grandma.
A maid her lifetime of winters, granddaughter of slaves.
Straight to my eyes:
"My mama used to tell me, one of these days
the hens gonna shit upwards!
And I'd stare at those hens' asses, wondering
when *will* that happen?
When we pushed the big ones down
and pulled the little ones up!"

"For Mama, Papa, and Blackie," she wrote
on the poem she left to say goodbye.
Nicaragua, 1977.
Disappear or be disappeared.
Dora Maria whose gaze
her mother always knew.
She trembled at her first delivery,
then took a city fearlessly.

Rain and the river rising, Catalina
chases her ducks that stray.
"And my months," she cries
on that platform with poles, a house
to do over and over.
"My months, gone in the hospital at Iquitos
and the full moon
bringing a madness to my head."
Her body is light against my touch.
A woman's voice, parting such density of rain.

Xuan, my cold hands in hers,
evokes the barracks.
"Soldiers who were our brothers."
Night after night, village by village.
Quang Tri, 1974.
Gunfire replaced by quiet conversation.
The work of women.
Xuan's history, too, is under attack.

Dominga brings her memory down
from the needle trade, Don Pedro,
her own babies dead from hunger.
"I want to tell you my story," she says,
"leave it to the young ones
so they'll know."
We are rocking. We are laughing.
This woman who rescued the flag at Ponce,
Puerto Rico, 1937.
Known by that act alone,
until a book carries her words. Her voice.

I bring you these women. Listen.
They speak, but their lives are under attack.

They too are denied adjustment of status
in the land of the free. In the home of the brave.

Winter, 1986

YOU DIDN'T MEAN IT PERSONALLY

I didn't mean it personally.

You don't say.

You didn't mean it personally?
Well then, exactly how *did* you mean it?

Impersonal
as a sudden knife against a throat?
Mind you, I am speaking of *any* throat: black, white, brown,
young, old, female, male.
A personal throat.

Impersonal as
the food
you have to eat / you must not eat,
it's just TV,
they're not talking to *you* you know.
You always take everything
so personally.

Impersonal as pain
eating another's belly
another's immune system
another's child?

Impersonal as chemicals
made so much more personal
when the right color,
a familiar surname is involved.

Impersonal as an unfamiliar shape
on a computerized map
hard to pronounce
impossible to see
or touch.
Impersonal as *their* war
until *our* boys
are threatened, missing, kidnapped, murdered.

Might you be talking about the personal monogram,
careful initials machine-stitched just for you
on the home-ec hankie, the polo shirt, or satin travel case
in which you can go anywhere
with that very personal diamond?

Can you guess where the stone
cut from South African rock
by South African shoulders, South African lungs,
stopped being hometown earth, became
your personal status symbol, beneath that monogram
or on your personal wrist?

And what about the wrist, personal when slapped, when held,
when touched:
when, by whom, under what concrete conditions?
What about your belly, your womb, your choice
personal or otherwise?
What about your space, sex, trust, language,
meaning of those rules?

You should be ashamed!
                          Oh, I didn't mean . . .
If you really loved him . . .
                          But I only meant . . .
It's not a matter of black and white . . .
                          I meant . . .
They're just workers!
                          I didn't mean . . .

They're just, you know,
it doesn't hurt *them* as much
to give up
their children,
their land,
their lives . . .

Well I meant . . . I mean, I didn't mean . . .
Well, you *do* know what I meant.
Don't you?

I know.
You didn't mean it personally.

I was afraid you did.

                                          Winter, 1988

BREAKING OUT

for Barbara

I

There were always those who had eyes to see
who understood the real meaning of *housemate*
deciphered the codes our words and hands spoke
across the distance a street   a room   a telephone wire.

We never said *lover* or *partner*
except by mistake
or within a silent circle, louder and spreading
as more trusted friends entered the safety of its space.

At first it was top secret
hugged to frightened breastbones
we vowed we would do this and more
for years   a lifetime if necessary.

They wanted me out because of what I speak, write,
because I won't say *I'm sorry*
or promise not to do it ever again.
And this love of ours is also branded deportable.

They wanted me out, and I fought   we fought
telling no one
as the circle enveloped a nation, a galaxy
burning out of sight.

II

Now that I've won this case, am judged a citizen
—was always one, they say—
I will claim, among other rights,
your name on my tongue.

This is my life partner I introduce you
in the restaurant parking lot. *I miss you*
I tell you on the phone, remembering
that was one of the phrases we sometimes allowed ourselves

when we turned the needles of pain to rage
and hoped that, blind to our womanlove,
they'd think we were just two friends
missing each other   missing each other so much.

Having come home, we are free to say our passion out loud
here on reclaimed land, identify ourselves,
share in the blasphemed freedom
enjoyed by every lesbian and gay man in the USA.

Summer, 1989

A VICTORY

for my son, Gregory

It's true, I wanted to come home
and the wanting grew high in me, though bogged
in memory, its knee-deep gasses
bloating silverfish. A rapid lurching
live about my legs.

Home. I knew the word but couldn't find its meaning.
Collapsed vowel, consonants screeching
in splintered dream.
Come and Go: interchangeable wounds
dead center of my breast.

Arms and legs followed the ancient center,
I was pulled along roads I did not recognize.
Today, entering the upgrade on my morning walk,
my body bends forward, left hand curled inward at the wrist,
fingers straining against left thigh.

Sky opens revealing brilliant salmon puffs, air
pungent of cedar
as fires are stoked to greet a closer day.
But oh that hand of mine, I stretch each finger,
and images

of Sharon Kowalski's dead hand's articulation
startle my eyes.
Where is the thinnest part,
always: Where is the weak link
giving before their deathway?

Yes, I came home. Knee-deep in bloodied limbs
and quiet dreams.
Now I carry the weakness and whole words
until their meaning stands in me
absent of shame. Wearing a new dress.

My skin bears witness to Jew and Arab
sharing a hope in Ramallah.
I sway and leap
in the streets of Johannesburg.
Ilopango. Ocotal. Bensonhurst. Valparaiso.

Home is a heart marked high and to the left
of childhood longing,
crouched against a sunken collarbone
but open. Naked
and beating with questions.

Still walking, still pushing ahead,
uphill hand pressed inarticulate
but sputtering against my thigh,
home parting and coming together
in light and sustenance. A constant victory.

Fall, 1989

CHRONOLOGY

1936
Margaret Randall is born in New York City. She is the oldest living child of Elinor Davidson Randall and John P. Randall who will have another daughter, Ann, and a son, John.

1939
In May, just four months before Hitler will invade Poland, the S.S. St. Louis approaches the coast of Florida with 907 German Jewish refugees. More than 700 of them have American sponsors and all their papers in order, except for a quota number. The U.S. Immigration Service refuses to allow the ship into port or the refugees to land. They are also refused by Cuba. After much negotiation, they are sent back to Europe where most manage to get into England, France or Belgium. Their fate is unknown.

1947
Randall's family moves to New Mexico. She is ten years old. Her father is a public school music teacher and her mother a Spanish-English translator. Elinor Randall's translation, over many years, of the works of the Cuban José Martí is a major literary accomplishment.

1948
First laws dealing with refugees result from increasing refugee populations generated by World War II. These include the Displaced Persons Act of 1948 and the Refugee Relief Act of 1953. On paper at least, a distinction is made between persons fleeing repressive governments and those seeking entrance for other reasons. All U.S. administrations, however, use immigration policy as an ideological weapon tied to political aims.

1952
McCarran-Walter Immigration and Nationality Act is passed by a McCarthyite Congress over President Truman's veto. The president's veto message states in part: "Seldom has a bill exhibited the distrust evidenced here for citizens and aliens alike." The act lists thirty-three provisions under which aliens may be prevented from entering, or expelled from, the United States. These include polygamy; mental illness; homosexuality; membership in communist, socialist or anarchist organizations; association with members of such organizations; and writing, speaking or disseminating opinions which dissent from official government views. In the main unmodified, this act has governed U.S. immigration for more than thirty-five years.

1955–56
Randall marries Sam Jacobs. Randall and her husband live and work in Seville, Spain.

1958–61
Randall, divorced from Jacobs, moves to New York City, where she begins to take her writing seriously.

1959
July, victory of Cuban Revolution.

Giant of Tears, Randall's first small book of poems, is self-published. In October, Randall gives birth to her first child, Gregory. His father is the poet Joel Oppenheimer.

1961
In September, Randall and her ten-month-old son leave the U.S. for Mexico. The circumstances of her life will keep Randall outside the country of her birth for the next twenty-three years. She will live mainly in Mexico, Cuba and Nicaragua.

1962–69
In January 1962, Randall, U.S. poet Harvey Wolin and Mexican poet Sergio Mondragon found *El Corno Emplumado/The Plumed Horn*, a bilingual literary quarterly which reflects the concerns of several generations of North and Latin American writers and acts as a bridge among varied modes of expression. It also publishes work by artists around the world. Wolin drops out after the second issue, Mondragon after seven years, while Randall continues to edit the publication, first alone and then with U.S. poet Robert Cohen. At the immigration hearing in 1986, INS will rely in part upon what is published in the magazine for its indictment of Randall.

1962
Randall and Mondragon marry in February.

1963
Daughter Sarah born in April.

1964
Reading tour of U.S. universities, with Sergio Mondragon. Daughter Ximena born in June.

1967
First trip to Cuba, to attend a meeting of poets honoring the one-hundredth anniversary of the birth of Nicaraguan modernist poet Ruben Dario.

While still married to Mondragon, and with two daughters from their union, Randall takes on the citizenship of her husband. He has not been able to provide for their family (which now consists of three children under the age of six, as well as the two adults), and she believes that she will be able to find better work if she becomes a Mexican. When she advises the U.S. consulate of her acquisition of Mexican nationality, she is told that she has lost her U.S. citizenship.

1968
Emergence of what has become known as the second wave of U.S. feminism. Randall makes a second trip to Cuba, to attend the Cultural Congress of Havana, a meeting of over six hundred Third World intellectuals.

Randall separates from Mondragon and begins to live with Robert Cohen.

July–October: Mexican student movement. Government shuts down protest with the massacre of more than one thousand students and citizens at the Plaza of Tlatelolco on October 2nd. The Olympic Games are held in Mexico later that month. Randall participates in the student movement and *El Corno Emplumado* supports movement demands.

1969
In March, gives birth to daughter Ana.

Realizing that she made a mistake in relinquishing U.S. citizenship, Randall attempts through an administrative recourse to recover her original nationality. She is turned down, with no reason given.

Randall and Mondragon are legally divorced. Political problems born of the 1968 Mexican student movement force Randall underground. With Cohen, she and her four children move to Cuba. She will live there for the next ten years.

1960s–1980s
The following are a few of the distinguished foreign artists, thinkers and statespersons who have been excluded from the United States by the state department or attorney general because of their political views or associations: Colombian author Gabriel García Marquez, English novelist Graham Greene, French actor Yves Montand, British politician Ian Paisley, Belgian sociologist Ernest Mandel, South African poet Dennis Brutus, Chilean president's widow Hortensia Buzzi de Allende, Canadian naturalist Farley Mowat, Argentine novelist Julio Cortazar, Nicaraguan minister of culture Ernesto Cardenal.

1972
Part of the Solution, a collection of poetry, prose and translations with an introduction by Robert Cohen, is published by New Directions, New York City. Poems and the introduction from this book will later be cited by INS lawyers as evidence against her. *La mujer cubana ahora*, Randall's first book on Cuban women, is published in Havana. Mexican, Canadian, Dutch, Venezuelan and Colombian editions will follow.

Randall travels to Chile, where she attends a Latin American meeting on women and witnesses the Chilean political process during the truck owners strike.

1973
September 11: Chilean coup. Agusto Pinochet takes power and initiates one of the worst massacres of civilian population in Latin American history. From September 1973 to January 1974, Randall spends several months in Peru, where she conducts a study on Peruvian women for the International Labor Office of the United Nations.

1974

On an invitation from the Vietnamese Women's Union, Randall visits the Socialist Republic of North Vietnam and Quang Tri in the liberated area below the 17th parallel.

1975

Publication of *Spirit of the People: Vietnamese Women Two Years from the Paris Accords* in both Mexico and Canada.

Randall and Cohen separate. Randall begins to live with Colombian poet Antonio Castro. They will be together for five years.

1976

Randall's *Doris Tijerino: Inside the Nicaraguan Revolution* appears in Canada. Mexican edition is *Somos millones*.

1977

McGovern Amendment to McCarran-Walter enacted. This is the only modification of any import that the act has suffered to date. The amendment states that temporary visas to aliens cannot be denied because of political beliefs or associations, and provides the possibility for a state department waiver in cases where such denials take place.

1978

Three-month-long reading and lecture tour of U.S. universities.

1979

July, victory of Sandinista revolution in Nicaragua.

Ernesto Cardenal, Nicaraguan minister of culture, invites Randall to visit and do field work for book on Nicaraguan women. She goes in September and stays until January 1980. Work will appear as the book *Sandino's Daughters*.

1980

Randall and Ana go to Nicaragua. A year later, Ximena joins them there. They will remain for three and a half years.

In the United States, the sanctuary movement begins. It is a massive grass-roots and largely religion-based movement to help refugees—most of them from El Salvador and Guatemala—who are fleeing the repressive regimes of those countries during long years of people's war. INS consistently tries to infiltrate the sanctuary movement, and many of those involved—including priests, ministers and religious sisters—are arrested and convicted. The most publicized trial will be that of eleven defendants in Tucson, Arizona, in 1985–86.

1981

Women in Cuba: Twenty Years Later, Randall's second book on Cuban women, is published in New York.

1982
Randall's *Breaking the Silences: 20th Century Poetry by Cuban Women* comes out in Canada.

1983
Christians in the Nicaraguan Revolution appears in Canada. A Nicaraguan edition is published a year later.

1984
In January, Randall returns to Albuquerque, New Mexico, the city where she grew up and which she identifies as home. In February, Randall and Floyce Alexander are married in Santa Fe. In March, at the Albuquerque INS office, Alexander petitions for Randall's permanent resident status. Later Randall's son, Gregory, makes a similar petition, and still later her mother, Elinor Randall, also does so. All the petitions are accepted by Immigration. Randall is told that she should have her green card in sixty to ninety days.

Randall's *Risking a Somersault in the Air: Conversations with Nicaraguan Writers* is published in San Francisco. In May, Congressman Barney Frank (D-Mass.) introduces H.R. #5227, to revise the grounds of exclusion under McCarren-Walter. Frank believes the test for exclusion should be one of "behavior which threatens public order." His bill fails to pass, and he re-introduces it in 1985. Although it has gained support, it has not yet been voted into law.

Randall is appointed adjunct assistant professor in American Studies, Women's Studies and English at the University of New Mexico in Albuquerque.

1985
Women Brave in the Face of Danger, a collection of Randall's photographs of North and Latin American women, with texts by women from two continents, is published in New York.

In June, Randall is called into the INS office in Albuquerque, where an inspector tapes a two-hour interview. A number of her books are opened and passages underlined; she is asked to explain her opinions. The Center for Constitutional Rights, a twenty-year-old human rights organization in New York City, agrees to take her case. The lawyers are David Cole, Michael Maggio, and Michael Ratner.

In October, although he does not find Randall's writings susceptible to the ideological exclusion clause of McCarren-Walter, INS district director A.L. Guigni uses his discretionary powers to deny her application for permanent resident status and gives her thirty days to leave the country.

1986
Randall's *Albuquerque: Coming Back to the USA* appears in Canada. In March, Senators Mathias and Simon introduce a bill which would modify the ideological exclusion and other clauses of McCarran-Walter. This

49

bill is not as broad as Barney Frank's, and both make special exclusion for members of the Palestine Liberation Organization. This bill is also still pending.

Throughout this year, Randall and many friends and supporters begin organizing her defense. The legal struggle is waged with some help from the ACLU. Many professional, academic, artistic and religious groups support the case. At one point twenty-five defense committees are working across the country.

From March 13–17, Randall has her five-day Immigration hearing in El Paso, Texas. Government attorneys, headed by Guadalupe Gonzalez, claim "Randall's writings are her own indictment against herself." They introduce nothing but those writings as evidence, and among other things accuse Randall of not ever having written a poem in praise of free enterprise, of having published anti–U.S. government cartoons in the literary magazine she edited in the 1960s, and of being "against the good order and happiness of the United States."

In August, Immigration Judge Martin F. Spiegel renders his decision. He concludes Randall should be barred from living in the U.S. permanently and orders her deported because, in his view, Randall's writings "advocate the economic, international and governmental doctrines of world communism." In his discretion he would allow her to stay, but he excludes her by applying McCarran-Walter.

In November, Randall and Barbara Byers begin living together.

1987
This Is About Incest, Randall's book about a personal experience with childhood sexual abuse, is published in New York.

In October's oral argument before the Board of Immigration Appeals in Washington, D.C., Randall's lawyers request termination of proceedings or adjustment of status.

In November, there is a hearing of Randall et al. against Edwin Meese, III, et al. This is the affirmative case brought by Randall with a number of other writers—among them Arthur Miller, Alice Walker, Norman Mailer, Toni Morrison, Kurt Vonnegut and William and Rose Styron. Judge John Penn, United States District Court for the District of Columbia, rules against the plaintiffs' application for a preliminary injunction.

In December, Congress enacts a one-year provision (Foreign Relations Authorization Act, 901(a)) that temporarily overrides much of the McCarran-Walter Act, including the section that affects Randall. Under this provision, "no alien may be denied a visa or excluded from admission into the United States . . . or be subject to deportation because of any past, current, or expected beliefs, statements, or associations which, if engaged in by a United States citizen in the U.S., would be protected under the Constitution of the United States."

Randall is appointed visiting professor of English at Trinity College in

Hartford, Connecticut.

1988

In January, a federal district court holds several deportation provisions of McCarran-Walter unconstitutional as applied to aliens living in the United States. The court holds that the First Amendment protects aliens living in the United States just as it protects citizens. The government appeals the decision.

In February, INS admits that 901 appears to resolve Randall's case, and that therefore she cannot be denied permanent resident status because of her writings. Case is still pending before the Board of Immigration Appeals. That same month, the United States Court of Appeals for the District of Columbia Circuit hears arguments on the affirmative case.

In August, Randall's children and grandchildren come from Cuba, Mexico, France and New York to spend a few weeks together in Albuquerque. Family reunion with four generations.

Randall's book of poems, *Memory Says Yes*, is published in Connecticut. *The Shape of Red: Insider/Outsider Reflections* by Ruth Hubbard and Randall is published in Pittsburgh.

In August, there is a decision on the affirmative case from the United States Court of Appeals for the District of Columbia Circuit. Judge Ruth B. Ginsburg writes negative majority opinion, with Judge Mikva writing favorable dissenting opinion.

In October, the Foreign Relations Appropriations Act 555 is passed. Congress makes changes in Section 901. It extends the legislation for two years, but limits its protection to aliens seeking non-immigrant (or non–permanent resident) visas. INS then revokes its prior position, arguing again that Randall should be denied permanent resident status and deported because of the "world communist" character of her writings.

That same month, the affirmative case goes to the Supreme Court of the United States, in its October 1988 term. The Supreme Court decides not to hear the case.

1989

During the spring semester, Randall is appointed Hubert H. Humphrey Visiting Professor of International Affairs at Macalester College in St. Paul, Minnesota.

As a result of the 1952 McCarran-Walter Immigration and Nationality Act, 50,000 people have been denied visas to enter the United States. In many cases they do not know this is so, nor upon what grounds, but their names appear in the now-computerized Lookout Book. The Lawyers' Committee for Human Rights sues to obtain the book under the Freedom of Information Act; a federal court in New York orders the government to produce it, but—so as not to compromise anybody's privacy—with all the names blacked out. The government doesn't hesitate to ask the court to reconsider its ruling.

In July, the Board of Immigration Appeals, in a surprise ruling, issues its decision on Randall's appeal from Judge Spiegel's deportation order. They find that Randall is still a U.S. citizen and should therefore never have been subjected to deportation proceedings in the first place. The BIA, in a 3–2 decision, finds that Randall did not voluntarily relinquish her U.S. citizenship when she became a Mexican citizen because she did so out of economic compulsion. The three BIA judges who rule in Randall's favor were appointed by Nixon and Ford; the two who dissent were appointed by Reagan.

The day of the decision, the government asks for, and is granted, a thirty-day stay in order to consider requesting a reversal by Attorney General Thornburgh. In August, INS finally desists in its pursuit of a reversal. The case is won. But in declaring Randall a U.S. citizen, the government has avoided the First Amendment issues of McCarran-Walter.

In September, a victory party is held in Berkeley, California; in October, one in Albuquerque, New Mexico; and in February 1990, in Amherst, Massachusetts.